The Original
Keto Diet Book

Simple, Healthy Recipes for Beginners and Pros
incl. 14-Day Meal Plan

[1st Edition]

William Slevens

Table of Contents

EXCLUSIVE BONUS!

Get Keto Audiobook for FREE NOW!*

*The Ultimate Keto Diet Guide 2019-2020:
How to Loose weight with Quick and Easy Steps*

SCAN ME

or go to

www.free-keto.co.uk

Introduction

Losing weight can be a challenge and keeping the weight off even more so. With so many options when it comes to this challenge, you may find it difficult to choose the right approach. If you are interested in one of the best ways to lose weight and keep it off, then you have probably checked out the keto diet. This cookbook is going to give you some delicious and amazing recipes that will help you on your weight loss journey.

However, before we dive into some of those tasty morsels, let's look at some of the basics when it comes to the keto diet.

What Is the Keto Diet?

This diet uses the low-carb, high-fat diet guidelines like many other successful diets, such as the Atkins diet. The difference is that, in the keto diet, the low-carb portion is taken even further. By reducing your carbohydrate intake and opting for more fat, you send your body into a natural metabolic state called ketosis.

This process helps your body work better at burning fat to use as your energy source. In turn, it also takes those fat cells and transforms them into ketones that reside in your liver. These ketones help generate food for your brain. This also lowers blood sugar and insulin levels, which provides a lot of great health benefits.

How to Lose Weight Effectively With the Keto Diet

You can reap some great benefits from utilizing the keto diet. If you want to get the most from this diet, there are also some tips that can help ensure the diet is being as effective as possible.

Here are some of those tips:

- **Reduce Your Carb Intake -** Setting your carb goal between 20 – 50 grams will help lower your blood sugar and insulin. This, of course, will get you into ketosis, which is the goal.

- **Coconut Oil -** This oil is rich in MCTs that help the ketones created in ketosis be absorbed quicker.

- **Feel the Burn -** By adding some extra exercise, you can promote even more ketone creation. You can even work out while fasting, which will increase the fat-burning effectiveness.

- **Healthy Fats -** The goal is to get about 60% of your calories from fats, as this will help boost ketone production. By choosing the right fats, you will be helping your overall health, as well. Hence, look for fats created from plants and animals.

- **Intermittent Fasting -** This process has you eating in a given time window, which is usually 8 – 10 hours. This will help your body get into ketosis faster.

- **Good Protein Levels -** If you don't get enough protein, then you may begin to lose muscle mass. Too much protein can hinder the efficiency of the diet, as well, so make sure you keep your protein levels just right.

How the Body Changes During the Keto Diet

As you get rolling on the keto diet, you will see a lot of changes occur both externally and internally. Here are some of the changes your body goes through while on the diet:

- **Rapid Weight Loss**
  - **Keto Flu** - This is caused by withdrawal symptoms from a lack of carb intake. You may experience a plethora of flu-like symptoms. Ride it out, it usually only lasts a few days.

  - **Muscle Cramps -** This is usually caused by a low level of sodium or potassium. If you experience this, you may want to add in a supplement or eat more foods with these minerals.

  - **Increased Insulin Sensitivity -** This may sound like a bad thing at first, but blood sugar levels rise higher when intaking a lot of carbs. This is actually bad and could cause health issues like diabetes. Without those carbs, your blood sugar will stay at manageable and efficient levels for your body.

- **Bad Breath -** You may experience some pretty rank breath, but, in some ways, that's a good thing. While in ketosis, our bodies› acetone creation rises, and this is expelled when we breathe. You may notice a metallic taste, as well as an odor.

There are other changes, like energy levels rising, inflammation decreasing, changes in your urine, and even stomach problems. However, the ones above are the most common.

How to Lose Up to 20 Pounds in 3 Weeks

The first step is to make sure you calculate your macros so that you have the right balance of fat, protein, and carbs for your body type, and be sure to set goals. Then, you will want to make sure to avoid the following mistakes:

- Make sure you are actually reaching ketosis. Make sure to test your ketone levels consistently. If you fall out of ketosis, then you can reduce your carb intake further and/or increase your fat intake.

- Make sure you know where your carbs are. There are foods that contain carbs that may be shocking to you. Make sure you stay away from processed foods and artificial sweeteners. Also, use a food tracker to keep an eye out for hidden carbs.

- Make sure you are eating the right amount of calories. This means tracking what you eat. Eating too little is just as bad as eating too much, so make sure you are staying in your sweet spot.

RECIPES

BREAKFAST

Homemade Sausage Patties

Ingredients:

- 1 lb. pork, ground (454g)
- 3/4 cup cheddar, shredded (63g)
- 1/4 cup buttermilk (59ml)
- 1 tbsp. onion, chopped
- 2 tsp. sage, ground
- 3/4 tsp. salt
- 3/4 tsp. pepper
- 1/8 tsp. garlic powder
- 1/8 tsp. oregano, dried

Directions:

1. In a bowl, combine all ingredients and stir together until thoroughly mixed. Shape into 1/2-inch thick patties and refrigerate for 60 minutes.

2. In a large cast-iron or nonstick skillet, cook patties over medium-high heat for 6-8 minutes per side or until nicely browned and serve.

Serves: 8

Nutritional Facts: Calories: 162 | Proteins: 13g | Carbs: 1g | Fats: 11g

Asparagus & Bacon Frittata

Ingredients:

- 12 oz. bacon (340g)
- 2 cups asparagus, cut into small pieces (303g)
- 1 cup onion, chopped (171g)
- 2 cloves garlic, minced
- 10 large eggs, beaten
- 1/4 cup parsley, chopped (27g)
- 1/2 tsp. salt
- 1/4 tsp. pepper
- 1 large tomato, diced small
- 1 cup cheddar, shredded (83g)

Directions:

1. In a large, oven-safe skillet, crisp bacon. Reserve 1 tbsp. drippings.

2. Take reserved drippings and heat on medium-high. Add the asparagus, onions, and garlic to skillet. Sauté until onions are translucent and garlic is fragrant. Break up the bacon and set a third of the bacon aside.

3. In a large mixing bowl, whisk together the bacon, eggs, parsley, salt, and pepper. Mix until eggs are frothy, pour into skillet. Top egg mixture with tomato, cheddar, and the remainder of the bacon. Cook, covered, over medium-low heat until the egg mixture is almost set.

4. Preheat broiler and place skillet under it. Cook until the top is lightly browned and serve.

Serves: 6

Nutritional Facts: Calories: 344 | Proteins: 23g | Carbs: 7g | Fats: 24g

Ham w/ Bacon, Mushroom, & Cheese

Ingredients:

- 2 tbsp. butter
- 1/2 lb. mushrooms, sliced (227g)
- 1 shallot, chopped fine
- 2 cloves garlic, minced
- 1/8 tsp. pepper
- 1 lb. ham steak, boneless, cut into 4 (454g)
- 1 cup Gruyere, shredded (83g)
- 4 bacon strips, cooked, crumbled
- 1 tbsp. parsley, fresh, chopped

Directions:

1. In a nonstick skillet, melt butter over medium-high heat. Add mushrooms and shallot and cook until softened. Then, add in garlic and pepper and cook until garlic is fragrant. Remove mixture and keep warm. Clean skillet.

2. Cook ham over medium heat in the same skillet. Flip steak and cover with cheese and bacon. Cook with lid on until cheddar is softened and ham is warmed through. Serve with mushroom mix spooned over top and sprinkle with parsley.

Serves: 4

Nutritional Facts: Calories: 352 | Proteins: 34g | Carbs: 5g | Fats: 22g

Frittata Stack

Ingredients:

- 8 large eggs
- 1/3 cup heavy whipping cream (237ml)
- 1/2 cup Romano, grated (53g)
- 1 1/2 tsp. salt
- 5 tbsp. olive oil
- 3/4 lb. mushrooms, sliced (340g)
- 1 medium onion, sliced thin
- 2 tbsp. basil, fresh, chopped
- 2 cloves garlic, minced
- 1/8 tsp. pepper
- 1 package Mascarpone

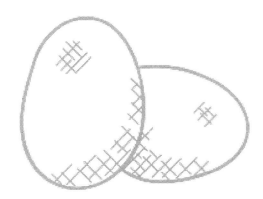

Directions:

1. Whisk eggs, cream, 1/4 cup (27g) Romano cheddar, and 1 tsp. salt in a large mixing bowl.

2. Heat 2 tbsp. oil over medium-high heat in a large skillet. When the oil is hot, add in mushrooms and onion. Cook until delicate or until tender, stirring occasionally. Then, add in basil, garlic, pepper, and salt. Cook for another minute or until you smell the garlic. Remove from skillet and stir in Mascarpone and leftover Romano.

3. Over medium-high heat, warm 1 tbsp. oil in the skillet. Ladle 1/3 of the egg mixture into skillet. Cook until mixture is set and then remove it to a platter. Tent with foil to keep warm. Repeat the process two more times.

4. Layer frittatas and mascarpone mixture on a platter until all layers are done, then top with remaining frittata. Cut into wedges and serve warm.

Serves: 6   Nutritional Facts: Calories: 468 | Proteins: 17g | Carbs: 6g | Fats: 44g

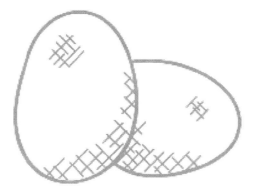

Florentine Casserole

Ingredients:

- 1 lb. sausage, pork (454g)
- 2 tbsp. butter
- 1 large onion, chopped
- 1 cup mushrooms, sliced (152g)
- 1 package spinach, frozen, defrosted, and squeezed

- 12 large eggs
- 2 cups of milk (473ml)
- 1 cup Swiss cheese, shredded (83g)
- 1 cup sharp cheddar, shredded (83g)

Directions:

1. Preheat your oven›s broiler to 350°F (177 C). Heat a large skillet over medium heat and then add sausage. Cook sausage until browned thoroughly and break up into small pieces as you cook. Drain grease and place in a baking dish that has been oiled.

2. Heat butter in a skillet over medium-high heat. Then, add onion and mushrooms. Cook until onions are translucent and mushrooms are tender. Mix in squeezed spinach. Cook for a minute and then spoon over sausage.

3. Whisk eggs and milk in a large mixing bowl until combined and eggs are frothy. Then, pour over mixture in baking dish. Top with cheese and sprinkle paprika. Place in oven and let bake for 30-35 minutes or until eggs are cooked through. Remove from oven and let stand. Then, cut and serve.

Serves: 12   Nutritional Facts: Calories: 271 | Proteins: 16g | Carbs: 6g | Fats: 20g

Quiche Cups w/ Broccoli

Ingredients:

- 1 cup broccoli, fresh, chopped (150g)
- 1 cup pepper jack cheese, shredded (83g)
- 6 large eggs
- 3/4 cup heavy whipping cream (177ml)
- 1/2 cup bacon bits (73g)
- 1 shallot, minced
- 1/4 tsp. salt
- 1/4 tsp. pepper

Directions:

1. Preheat oven to 350°F (177 C). Oil a muffin tin and then divide broccoli and cheddar between the cups.

2. Combine the rest of ingredients into a large mixing bowl and whisk until combined thoroughly. Distribute egg mixture among muffin cups. Place in oven and bake until eggs are cooked through and set. Serve.

Serves: 6   Nutritional Facts: Calories: 291 | Proteins: 16g | Carbs: 4g | Fats: 24g

Oven-Baked Denver Omelette

Ingredients:

- 8 large eggs
- 1/2 cup half-and-half (118ml)
- 1 cup cheddar, shredded (83g)
- 1 cup ham, cooked, chopped (182g)
- 1/4 cup bell pepper, green, chopped
- 1/4 cup onion, chopped

Directions:

1. Whisk eggs and cream together in a large mixing bowl. Then, add in the remaining ingredients and stir until combined. Pour into a buttered baking dish.

2. Preheat oven to 400°F (204 C). Then, place the baking dish in the oven and bake for 25 minutes or until the top is golden brown. Remove, let stand for a few minutes to cool, then cut and serve.

Serves: 6

Nutritional Facts: Calories: 235 | Proteins: 17g | Carbs: 4g | Fats: 16g

Scrambled Eggs w/ Avocado

Ingredients:

- 8 large eggs
- 1/2 cup milk, whole (118ml)
- 1/2 tsp. salt
- 1/4 tsp. pepper

- 1 medium avocado, peeled, cubed
- 2 tbsp. butter
- 6 slices of bacon, cooked, crumbled

Directions:

1. Beat eggs in a large mixing bowl and then add in the remaining ingredients. Stir until combined. Then, add the mixture to a heated large skillet and cook, stirring frequently. When scrambled to your liking, remove and serve with bacon crumbled over top.

Serves: 6

Nutritional Facts: Calories: 233 | Proteins: 12g | Carbs: 4g | Fats: 19g

Egg & Bacon Bundles

Ingredients:

- 12 slices of bacon
- 1 tsp. butter
- 6 large eggs
- ¼ tsp. pepper

Directions:

1. Preheat oven to 325°F (163 C). Cook bacon slices in a large skillet until partly cooked. Remove and drain on paper towels.

2. Butter a 6-cup muffin tin and place two halves of one slice of bacon on the bottom of each cup. Then, wrap one whole bacon slice around the inside of the muffin cup. Crack one egg into each cup.

3. Place in oven and cook for 12-18 minutes or until the whites have set. Remove from oven and sprinkle with salt and pepper.

Serves: 6   Nutritional Facts: Calories: 311 | Proteins: 13g | Carbs: 1g | Fats: 28g

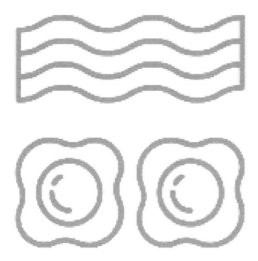

Greek-Inspired Breakfast Casserole

Ingredients:

- 1/2 lb. Italian turkey sausages, removed from casings (227g)
- 1/2 cup bell pepper, green, chopped (85g)
- 1 shallot, chopped
- 1 small can artichoke hearts, drained, washed, chopped
- 1 cup broccoli, fresh, chopped (150g)
- 1/3 cup sun-dried tomatoes, chopped (50g)
- 6 large eggs
- 6 large egg whites
- 3 tbsp. milk, non-fat
- 1/2 tsp. Italian seasoning
- 1/4 tsp. garlic powder
- 1/4 tsp. pepper
- 1/3 cup feta, crumbled

Directions:

1. Preheat oven to 350°F (177 C). Cook sausage, pepper, and shallot in a large skillet over medium heat until sausage is browned. Stir and break up sausage while doing this. Then, remove mixture and place in a buttered baking dish. Sprinkle over top the artichokes, broccoli, and sun-dried tomatoes.

2. Combine in a large mixing bowl the eggs, egg whites, milk, and seasonings. Then, whisk until completely combined. Pour over mixture in baking dish. Top with feta.

3. Bake uncovered until eggs are thoroughly set, about 45-50 minutes. Remove, let cool, and then serve.

Serves: 6   Nutritional Facts: Calories: 179 | Proteins: 17g | Carbs: 8g | Fats: 9g

Hazelnut Scones w/ Chocolate Chips

Ingredients:

- 2 1/2 cups flour, hazelnut
- 1/2 cup flour, flaxseed
- 1/3 cup sugar substitute of choice
- 1 tbsp. baking powder
- 1/4 tsp. salt
- 2 large eggs

- 1/4 cup oil, hazelnut
- 2 tbsp. cream
- 1/2 tsp. extract, vanilla
- 1/4 tsp. stevia
- 1/3 cup chocolate chips, sugar-free

Directions:

1. Preheat oven to 325 F (163 C). Line a baking sheet with parchment paper.

2. Whisk together the flour, sugar, salt, and baking powder. Then, add in eggs, oil, cream, and extract. Mix until batter comes together. Then, add in chocolate chips.

3. Pour mixture out onto the baking sheet and form batter into a square (about 1" thick [2.5cm]) Use a sharp blade to cut into 6 even squares. Then, cut diagonally to form triangles.

4. Separate them carefully and place them on a baking sheet. Space evenly on baking sheet. Place in oven and bake for 20-25 minutes or until firm to the touch and lightly browned.

5. Remove from the stove and let cool before serving.

Serves: 12

Nutritional Facts: Calories: 323 | Proteins: 7g | Carbs: 12g | Fats: 28g

Bagel Keto-Style

Ingredients:

- 1 cup flour, coconut (96g)
- 1/4 cup fiber, psyllium (24g)
- 1/2 cup sesame seeds (142g)
- 1/2 cup hemp hearts (73g)
- 1/2 cup pumpkin seeds (36g)
- 6 egg whites
- 1 tsp. sea salt
- 1 tbsp. baking powder

Directions:

1. Preheat oven to 350 F (177 C). Combine all dry ingredients into a large mixing bowl thoroughly.

2. Whisk the egg whites until frothy in a medium mixing bowl. Then, combine the egg whites into the dry ingredients. Mix well with a spoon. The dough should be crumbly. Now, add in 1 cup (237ml) of hot water to the mixture and mix until the dough comes together.

3. Line a baking sheet with parchment paper and roll the dough into 6 balls. While holding the ball in one hand, use your thumb to create the bagel hole. Then, place onto the baking sheet and finish forming your bagel. Now, top with nut mixture.

4. Bake in the oven for about an hour. Then, let bagels cool before serving.

Serves: 6

Nutritional Facts: Calories: 352 | Proteins: 18g | Carbs: 8g | Fats: 19g

Stuffed Waffles w/ Ham & Cheese

Ingredients:

- 7 tbsp. almond milk, unsweetened
- 1/2 tsp. vinegar, apple cider
- 2 large eggs
- 1 tbsp. coconut oil
- 1/2 tsp. vanilla extract
- 3/4 cup flour, almond (72g)
- 2 1/2 tbsp. flour, coconut
- 2 tsp. baking powder
- 2 tsp. preferred sweetener
- 4 slices ham, deli
- 4 slices cheese of your choice

Directions:

1. Preheat waffle iron and spray it with nonstick cooking spray.

2. Combine almond milk and vinegar in a large mixing bowl. Then, add eggs, coconut oil, and vanilla extract to the mixture and whisk until thoroughly combined. Set to the side.

3. In another mixing bowl, combine all the dry ingredients. Then, add to egg mixture. Whisk until combined well.

4. Pour a quarter of the mixture into a waffle iron. Then, place 2 slices of ham and cheese each. Pour in more batter until covered. Close iron and cook for 3-5 minutes or until steam can't be seen from the waffle iron. Remove carefully and serve.

Serves: 4   Nutritional Facts: Calories: 350 | Proteins: 21g | Carbs: 6g | Fats: 25g

Bacon Cheese Rolls

Ingredients:

- 5 oz. bacon, diced (142g)
- 2 tbsp. cream cheese
- 2 tbsp. sesame seeds
- 1 tbsp. psyllium husk
- 1/2 tsp. baking powder

- 1 cup cheese, cheddar, shredded (83g)
- 1/2 cup mozzarella, shredded (42g)
- 3 eggs
- 1/2 tsp. pepper
- 1 pinch salt

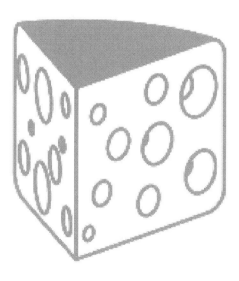

Directions:

1. Preheat oven to 355 F (180 C). In a large skillet over medium heat, add and sauté the bacon until just browned. Set aside a little bacon. Remove from heat and add the cream cheese to the remaining bacon and let cool for about 5 minutes.

2. Place bacon/cream cheese mixture into your food processor and add in the remaining ingredients. Pulse on medium for 3-5 minutes or until ingredients are thoroughly combined. In 12 even piles, spoon out mixture on a parchment-lined baking sheet. Sprinkle extra bacon on each roll.

3. Bake for 13-16 minutes or until the rolls are light golden brown and have risen. Then, remove from oven and serve.

Serves: 12   Nutritional Facts: Calories: 149 | Proteins: 9g | Carbs: 2g | Fats: 12g

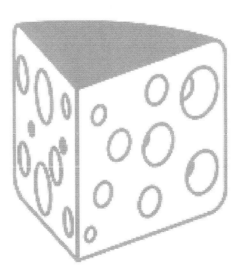

Radish & Cauliflower Hash Browns w/ Bacon

Ingredients:

- 1 lb. radishes, shredded (454g)
- 3 cups cauliflower, riced (410g)
- 3 cloves garlic, minced
- Salt & pepper to taste
- 1/2 tsp. paprika, smoked
- 3 tbsp. olive oil
- 6 slices of bacon, cooked and crumbled

Directions:

1. Mix together in a large bowl, the radishes, cauliflower, salt, pepper, and paprika. Blend until all ingredients are combined thoroughly.

2. In a large skillet, heat oil over medium-high heat. When the oil is hot, layer hash brown mixture over the entire bottom of the skillet.

3. Toss in the bacon crumbles and fry until the hash browns are cooked through, around 20-30 minutes. Stir as required. Taste and add salt and pepper as needed. Then, serve with eggs garnished with parsley.

Serves: 4

Nutritional Facts: Calories: 196 | Proteins: 7g | Carbs: 9g | Fats: 15g

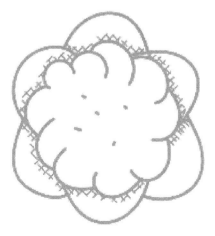

LUNCH

Fish Cakes w/ Lemon Avocado Sauce

Ingredients:

- Cake
- 1 lb. white fish, raw, boneless (454g)
- 1/4 cup cilantro (27g)
- Pinch of salt
- Pinch of chili flakes
- 2 cloves garlic, chopped fine
- 2 tbsp. oil, coconut
- Sauce
- 2 avocados, ripe
- 1 lemon, juiced
- Pinch of salt
- 2 tbsp. water

Directions:

1. Add all fish cake ingredients into a food processor and pulse until completely combined.

2. Heat the oil in a large skillet over medium-high heat. Coat hands with oil and form fish mixture into cakes until mix is gone. Place cakes into skillet and cook until nicely browned and cooked through.

3. While cakes are cooking, add all ingredients of sauce into a processor and pulse until smooth and rich. Taste the blend and add more lemon juice or salt if needed. Serve warm with sauce for dipping.

Serves: 6   Nutritional Facts: Calories: 69 | Proteins: 1g | Carbs: 2.7g | Fats: 6.5g

Spiced Coconut Chicken

Ingredients:

- 2 tbsp. oil, coconut
- 1 yellow onion, sliced
- 5 cloves garlic, minced
- 1-inch fresh ginger, sliced (2.5cm)
- 2 tsp. turmeric, ground
- 1 tbsp. garam masala
- 1 tbsp. cumin, ground
- 1 tsp. chili powder
- 1 tsp. salt
- 1/2 tsp. pepper
- 1/2 tsp. cayenne
- 1/2 tsp. cinnamon, ground
- 2 lbs. chicken breast, boneless, skinless, cubed (907g)
- 1 can coconut milk
- 1 can tomato sauce
- 1 cinnamon stick
- 2 tbsp lemon juice, fresh
- 2 cups frozen green beans (218g)
- ¼ cup cilantro, fresh, chopped (27g)

Directions:

1. In a large skillet, heat oil. Cook onion and garlic until translucent and fragrant, around 5 minutes. Then, add ginger, chili powder, garam masala, turmeric, cumin, salt, pepper, cinnamon, and cayenne and mix. Cook for another 1-2 minutes.

2. Move onion/garlic mix to slow cooker. Then, add chicken, cinnamon, tomato sauce, coconut milk, and lemon juice to the slow cooker, as well. Cover and cook on low for 6 hours. With 1 hour, left add green beans to the cooker.

3. Serve over cauliflower rice garnished with cilantro and a wedge of lemon.

Serves: 8   Nutritional Facts: Calories: 304 | Proteins: 28g | Carbs: 9g | Fats: 18g

Asian Meatballs w/ Vinaigrette

Ingredients:

Meatballs

- 1 lb. beef, ground (450g)
- 1 tbsp. ginger, fresh grated
- 1 tbsp. scallions
- 3 cloves garlic, chopped
- 1 tbsp. tamari
- 1 tsp. sesame oil
- 1 egg

Sauce

- 3 tbsp. tamari
- 3 cloves garlic, chopped
- 1 tbsp. scallions
- 1 tsp. vinegar
- 1 tsp. sesame oil

Directions:

1. Preheat oven to 400 F (200 C).

2. Combine all meatball ingredients into a bowl and mix well. Form mixture into balls and place on an oiled baking sheet. Place in oven and bake for 18-22 minutes or until cooked through.

3. Combine all the sauce ingredients into one bowl and mix well. When meatballs are done, remove from oven and let sit for 5 minutes. Then, serve with sauce.

Serves: 2

Nutritional Facts: Calories: 620 | Proteins: 52g | Carbs: 11g | Fats: 43g

Tortilla Espanola

Ingredients:

- 1 1/2 cups olive oil, extra virgin(350ml)
- 1 medium onion, sliced
- 1 1/2lbs. radishes, sliced thin (700g)
- 8 eggs
- Salt and pepper for taste
- Parsley, fresh, chopped

Directions:

1. Heat olive oil over medium heat in a large skillet. Turn down heat to low and add the radish and onion. Sprinkle salt as you layer the radishes and onions into the skillet. Mix every so often until completely cooked. Do not brown the radishes or onions.

2. In a medium mixing bowl, add eggs and a nice pinch of salt. Whisk until combined and set to the side.

3. Drain radishes and onions and allow to cool. Preheat oven to 350°F (180°C). Clean skillet and coat with oil. Pour in egg and radish blend and cook until the sides start to set.

4. Remove from heat, sprinkle with parsley, and bake until eggs completely set. Let rest for 10 minutes. Cut and serve.

Serves: 8

Nutritional Facts: Calories: 159 | Proteins: 6g | Carbs: 4g | Fats: 13g

Zucchini Noodles w/ Shrimp

Ingredients:

- 2 tbsp. butter, unsalted
- 2 tbsp. olive oil
- 1 lb. medium shrimp, peeled and deveined (454g)
- 1 shallot, minced
- 4 cloves garlic, minced
- 1/4 tsp. red pepper flakes
- Salt and pepper for taste
- 1/4 cup vegetable stock (59ml)
- 2 tbsp. lemon juice, fresh
- 1 tsp. zest, lemon
- 1/2 lb. zucchini, spiralized (227g)
- 2 tbsp. Parmesan, grated

Directions:

1. Combine butter and olive oil in a large skillet over medium-high heat. Then, add the shrimp, shallots, garlic, and red pepper flakes. Add salt and pepper for taste. Stir gently as you cook the mixture. Do this until shrimp is pink and cooked through.

2. Add in vegetable stock, lemon juice, and lemon zest. Season with salt and pepper for taste. Simmer and then stir in zucchini noodles until warmed through, around 1-2 minutes. Serve with Parmesan sprinkled on top.

Serves: 4

Nutritional Facts: Calories: 235 | Proteins: 17g | Carbs: 9g | Fats: 16g

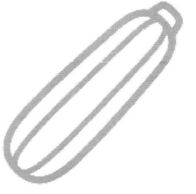

Cucumber Avocado Chicken Salad

Ingredients:

- 1 rotisserie chicken, shredded
- 1 large cucumber, sliced
- 5 large tomatoes, chopped
- 1/4 onion, red, sliced thin
- 2 avocados, diced
- ½ cup parsley, fresh, chopped (53g)
- 3 tbsp. olive oil
- 3 tbsp. lemon juice, fresh
- Salt and pepper for taste

Directions:

1. Combine all the ingredients together in one large mixing bowl. Then, gently drizzle the olive oil and lemon juice over the mixture. Add salt and pepper for taste and then toss.

Serves: 6

Nutritional Facts: Calories: 545 | Proteins: 40g | Carbs: 10g | Fats: 38g

Low-Carb Cauliflower Salad

Ingredients:

- 2 heads of cauliflower, cut into florets
- 2 tbsp. olive oil
- 1/2 tsp. salt
- 1/4 tsp. pepper
- 1 1/2 cups avocado mayonnaise (225g)

- 1/4 cup mustard (62.3g)
- 1 cup pickles, dill, chopped (143g)
- 1 cup onion, chopped (160g)
- 1/2 cup celery, diced (51g)
- 6 large eggs, hard-boiled
- 1 tbsp. vinegar, apple cider
- Paprika

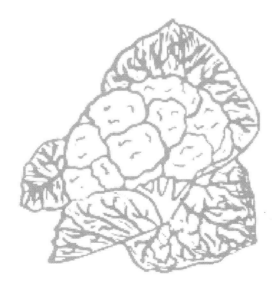

Directions:

1. Preheat the oven to 375° F(191 C). Line two baking sheets with parchment paper.

2. Chop the cauliflower into small sections and coat with olive oil, salt, and pepper. Spread in an even layer over baking sheets. Place in oven and bake for half an hour (flipping part of the way through) until the tops lightly browned. Let the cauliflower cool. Boil your eggs while the cauliflower is cooking.

3. Combine the rest of the ingredients together, including the cauliflower and 4 diced eggs, in a large mixing bowl. Season with salt and pepper to taste. Place in serving platter and place the rest of the eggs cut on top. Sprinkle with paprika, chill until ready to serve.

Serves: 12   Nutritional Facts: Calories: 302 | Proteins: 5g | Carbs: 7g | Fats: 27g

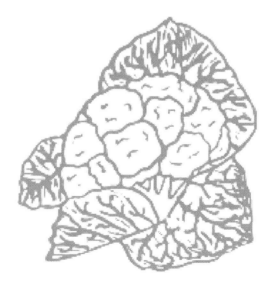

Egg Salad w/ Avocado

Ingredients:

- 6 eggs, boiled, diced
- 2 avocados, diced
- 1/2 lemon, juiced
- 1/4 cup onions, diced (43g)

- 2 tsp. dill, fresh
- 1/2 tsp. salt
- 1/2 tsp. pepper

Directions:

1. Add all the eggs and avocado into a mixing bowl and stir until creamy. Then, add in herbs and seasoning. Squeeze lemon over the mixture and mix until combined thoroughly. Then, serve.

Serves: 6

Nutritional Facts: Calories: 160 | Proteins: 7g | Carbs: 6g | Fats: 12g

Green Bean & Roasted Fennel Salad

- ◆ 2 medium fennel bulbs
- ◆ 1 tbsp. olive oil
- ◆ 14 oz. green beans, fresh (400g)
- ◆ 1/3 cup parsley, fresh, chopped (35g)
- ◆ 1/2 tbsp. lemon juice, fresh

- ◆ 2 tsp. capers
- ◆ 1/4 cup olive oil (59ml)
- ◆ 1/4 tsp. pepper
- ◆ 1/2 tsp. salt
- ◆ 1/3 cup almonds, toasted and sliced (36g)

Directions:

1. Preheat the oven to 350 F (175 C). Then, slice fennel bulbs and lay out on a large baking sheet. Coat with olive oil and place in the oven to bake for 20 minutes or until lightly browned.

2. Heat a pot of water until boiling. Add in green beans and cook until crisp but flexible. Then, drain and rinse with cold water to halt cooking.

3. Add the rest of the ingredients, excluding the almonds, into a food processor and pulse until the parsley is broken into little bits.

4. Then, add fennel, green beans, and almonds into a large mixing bowl and pour dressing over. Toss to coat and then serve.

Serves: 4

Nutritional Facts: Calories: 247 | Proteins: 3g | Carbs: 14g | Fats: 18g

Shrimp & Cauliflower Rice Salad

Ingredients:

Salad

- 4 cups cauliflower, riced (713g)
- 2 cups shrimp, cooked and sliced in half (303g)
- 1 cup cabbage, red (83g)
- 1/4 cup basil, fresh, chopped (27g)
- 2 tbsp. zest, pink grapefruit

Dressing

- 1/4 cup pink grapefruit juice, fresh (59ml)
- 3 tbsp. oil, avocado
- 2 tbsp. vinegar, apple cider
- 3 tbsp. sugar substitute of choice
- 1/2 tsp. pepper
- 1 tsp. salt

Directions:

1. In a large mixing bowl, combine all the salad ingredients. Then, in a small food processor, toss in all the dressing ingredients and blend until smooth.

2. Pour over salad and mix until thoroughly coated. Serve.

Serves: 6

Nutritional Facts: Calories: 143 | Proteins: 9g | Carbs: 5g | Fats: 10g

Romaine Lettuce Soup

Ingredients:

- ½ small onion, diced
- 2 cloves garlic, minced
- 3 tbsp. coconut oil, butter flavored
- 1 tbsp. basil, fresh, chopped
- 1 tbsp. parsley, fresh, chopped
- 1 tsp. salt
- 1/8 tsp. pepper
- 2 cups cauliflower, chopped (214g)
- 8 cups romaine lettuce, chopped (376g)
- 4 cups chicken broth (946ml)

Directions:

1. In a large skillet, heat coconut oil and add in onion and garlic. Sauté until translucent and fragrant. Then, add in seasoning and cook for another few minutes. Now, add in all the remaining ingredients and simmer for about 15 minutes.

2. In batches, use your blender to blend mixture until smooth, return to pot, and cook for another few minutes. Add salt and pepper for taste and then serve.

Serves: 8

Nutritional Facts: Calories: 73 | Proteins: 1g | Carbs: 4g | Fats: 6g

Instant Noodle Cups

Ingredients:

- 3 tsp. miso paste
- 3 tsp. tamari
- 1/4 cup mushrooms, sliced (38g)
- 1/4 cup kale (15g)
- 3/4 cup udon, cooked (82g)
- ¼ cup bean sprouts (21g)
- 1/4 cup fresh herbs (cilantro, basil, parsley, etc.) (27g)

Directions:

1. Layer all ingredients from the top to the bottom in a mason jar. When ready top with hot water. Then, replace the lid and let steep for a few minutes.

2. Then, stir thoroughly and eat.

Serves: 2

Nutritional Facts: Calories: 79 | Proteins: 4g | Carbs: 15.2g | Fats: 1.3g

Cauliflower & Turmeric Soup

Ingredients:

- 1 large head cauliflower, cut into chunks
- 1/2 large carrot, chopped
- 1-inch ginger piece, fresh, chopped (2.5cm)
- 2 tbsp. turmeric, ground
- 1 tsp. pepper
- 2 tsp. salt
- 1 cup coconut milk (237ml)

Directions:

1. Boil 8 cups of water in a large stockpot. Then, add in the cauliflower, carrot, and ginger. Simmer for about 20 minutes and then turn down the heat. Cook until vegetables are soft.

2. Then, turn off the heat and begin dividing the soup into batches, using your blender to puree the soup in stages. Then, turn the heat back on and add in the remaining ingredients. Stir and let cook for another 5 minutes. Then, let cool for 5 minutes and serve topped with your favorite toppings and garnishes.

Serves: 6

Nutritional Facts: Calories: 96 | Proteins: 3g | Carbs: 7g | Fats: 2g

Avocado Cucumber Gazpacho

Ingredients:

- 2 medium cucumbers, peeled, seeded, and chopped
- 1 1/2 avocados, chopped
- 1 jalapeno, chopped
- 1/3 cup cilantro, chopped (35g)
- 1/4 cup vinegar, apple cider (59ml)
- 2 cloves garlic, chopped
- 1 tsp. salt
- 3/4 tsp. pepper
- 1 1/2 cups water (356ml)

Directions:

1. Combine all ingredients into a blender and blend until smooth. Add water as needed to thin the mixture out. Then, add salt and pepper for taste. Then, serve.

Serves: 6   Nutritional Facts: Calories: 95 | Proteins: 2g | Carbs: 8.3g | Fats: 6.3g

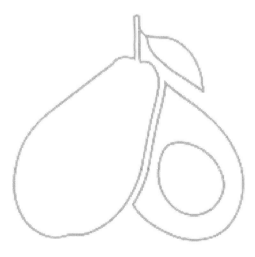

Creamy Chicken Soup

Ingredients:

- 8 1/2 cups water (2L)
- 1 whole chicken
- 2 tbsp. vinegar, apple cider
- 3 1/2 cups pumpkin, fresh, cubed (525g)
- 1 lime, juiced
- 2 tbsp. ginger, fresh, chopped fine
- 2 medium zucchinis
- 1/2 cup parsley, fresh, chopped (53g)
- 1/2 cup cilantro, fresh, chopped (53g)
- 2 tsp. turmeric, ground
- 1 cup coconut cream (237ml)
- 2 tsp. salt
- 2 shallots, chopped
- 4 cloves garlic, chopped
- 1 tsp. chili flakes
- Pepper for taste

Directions:

1. In a slow cooker, add the chicken and cover with water and apple cider vinegar. Cook on low for 4 hours or until chicken begins to pull off the bone.

2. Remove chicken from the slow cooker and strain broth from fragments. Then, return to slow cooker and add in pumpkin, zucchini, and ginger. Simmer on low for 15 minutes or until veggies are tender. Then, pull chicken off the bone and set aside.

3. Then, add the rest of the ingredients into the slow cooker with vegetables. Let heat all the way through. Then, add salt and pepper for taste. Serve hot with toppings of your liking.

Serves: 6

Nutritional Facts: Calories: 170 | Proteins: 6g | Carbs: 7.3g | Fats: 14g

DINNER

Fried Chicken

Ingredients:

Chicken

- ♦ 6 chicken breast, bone-in, skin-on
- ♦ Salt and pepper for taste
- ♦ 2 large eggs
- ♦ 1/2 cup heavy cream (118ml)
- ♦ 3/4 cup flour, almond (72g)
- ♦ 1 1/2 cup pork rinds, crushed (160g)
- ♦ 1/2 cup Parmesan, grated (100g)
- ♦ 1 tsp.garlic powder
- ♦ 1/2 tsp. paprika

Mayo

- ♦ 1/2 cup mayonnaise (108g)
- ♦ 1 1/2 tsp. hot sauce

Directions:

1. Preheat oven to 400°F (204 C). Then, take some parchment paper and line a baking sheet. Dry chicken with paper towels and then season both sides with salt and pepper.

2. Combine eggs and heavy cream in a large mixing bowl and whisk together. Then, in another bowl, combine flour, pork rinds, Parmesan, and paprika.

3. In batches, dredge chicken in the egg mix and then add the flour blend. Place on a lined baking sheet. Repeat until all the chicken is coated. Bake until chicken is browned or until chicken is baked through.

4. While the chicken is baking, combine sauce ingredients in a small mixing bowl and stir until combined thoroughly.

5. Serve chicken warm with sauce.

Serves: 8   Nutritional Facts: Calories: 109 | Proteins: 4g | Carbs: 3.3g | Fats: 9g

Meatballs in Sauce

Ingredients:

Meatballs

- 1 lb. beef, ground (545g)
- 1 clove garlic. minced
- 1/2 cup mozzarella, shredded (42g)
- 1/4 cup Parmesan, grated (50g)
- 2 tbsp. parsley, fresh, chopped
- 1 large egg
- 1 tsp. salt
- 1/2 tsp. pepper
- 2 tbsp. olive oil, extra virgin

Sauce

- 1 medium onion, chopped
- 2 cloves garlic, minced
- 1 can crushed tomatoes
- 1 tsp. oregano, dried
- Salt and pepper for taste

Directions:

1. Combine meat, garlic, mozzarella, Parmesan, parsley, egg, salt, and pepper in a large mixing bowl. Mix well and form meat mixture into balls.

2. Heat the oil in a large skillet over medium heat. Place balls in the hot skillet and cook, turning frequently until meatballs are browned. Remove from skillet and let drain on a paper towel-lined platter.

3. In the skillet, add in onion and cook until translucent. Then, add garlic and cook until fragrant. Now, you can add in the tomatoes and oregano and season with salt and pepper.

4. Place meatballs back into the sauce and cook for another 15 minutes. Then, remove from heat and serve topped with Parmesan.

Serves: 4   Nutritional Facts: Calories: 357 | Proteins: 37.7g | Carbs: 12.4g | Fats: 17.4g

Garlicky Pork Chops w/ Rosemary

Ingredients:

- 4 pork chops
- Salt and pepper for taste
- 1 tbsp. rosemary, fresh, minced
- 2 cloves garlic, minced
- 1 stick butter, melted
- 1 tbsp. olive oil, extra virgin

Directions:

1. Preheat oven to 375 F (191 C). Season both sides of the chops liberally with salt and pepper. Combine butter, rosemary, and garlic together in a small mixing bowl. Then, set to the side.

2. Heat olive oil in an oven-safe skillet over medium-high heat. Then, add pork and sear on both sides until golden. Then, brush the butter mixture over each chop.

3. Place skillet in the heated oven and let them cook for 12 minutes. Then, top with more garlic butter.

Serves: 4   Nutritional Facts: Calories: 547 | Proteins: 40.6g | Carbs: 1g | Fats: 40.1g

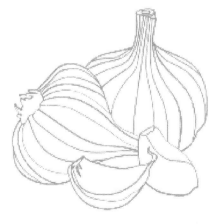

Taco Casserole

Ingredients:

- 1 tbsp. olive oil, extra virgin
- 1/2 onion, diced
- 2 lbs. beef, ground (907g)
- 2 tbsp. salt
- Pepper for taste

- 2 tbsp. taco seasoning
- 1 jalapeno, minced
- 6 large eggs
- 2 cup parsley, fresh, chopped (213g)
- 1 cup sour cream (215g)

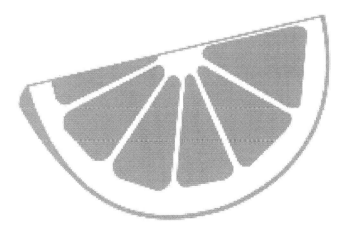

Directions:

1. Preheat oven to 350°F (177 C). Heat the oil in a large skillet over medium heat. Then, add onion and cook until soft. Add in beef and season with salt and pepper. Cook until brown, breaking up meat as you cook it. Add in taco seasoning and jalapeno. Cook until all the flavors combine. Remove from heat, drain, and let cool.

2. Whisk eggs in a large mixing bowl and, once done, add-in cooked beef. Spread the mixture in an even layer over the bottom of a Dutch oven. Then, sprinkle the top with cheese.

3. Bake until set, around 25 minutes. Sprinkle with parsley and top with a dab of sour cream and jalapeño.

Serves: 6

Nutritional Facts: Calories: 583 | Proteins: 53.3g | Carbs: 5.7g | Fats: 37g

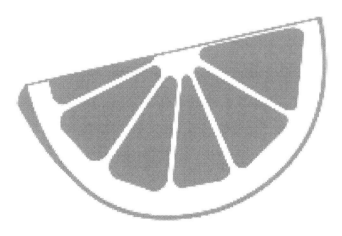

Meatloaf

Ingredients:

- Nonstick cooking spray
- 1 tbsp. olive oil, extra-virgin
- 1 medium onion, chopped
- 1 stalk celery, chopped
- 3 cloves garlic, minced
- 1 tsp. oregano, dried
- 1 tsp. chili powder
- 2 lb. beef, ground (907g)

- 1 cup cheddar, shredded (83g)
- 1/2 cup flour, almond (48g)
- 1/4 cup Parmesan, grated (27g)
- 2 eggs
- 1tbsp. soy sauce, low-sodium
- Salt and pepper for taste
- 6 strips of bacon

Directions:

1. Preheat oven to 400°F (204 C). Coat a medium baking dish with cooking spray. Heat the oil in a skillet over medium heat and then add onion and celery. Cook until vegetables are softened. Then, mix in garlic, oregano, and chili powder. Cook until fragrant. Let the mixture cool.

2. Combine beef, vegetable blend, cheese, flour, eggs, and soy sauce. Then, season with salt and pepper. Mix well and then shape into a meatloaf within the oiled baking dish. Then, lay the bacon slices over the top of the meat-loaf.

3. Bake in the oven until the bacon is crisp. This should take about an hour. Remove and let cool for a minute and then slice and serve.

Serves: 6

Nutritional Facts: Calories: 507 | Proteins: 51g | Carbs: 5.1g | Fats: 30.2g

Lemon Garlic Mahi-Mahi

Ingredients:

- 3 tbsp. butter, divided
- 2 tbsp. olive oil, extra-virgin
- 4 mahi-mahi filets
- Salt and pepper for taste
- 1 lb. asparagus (454g)
- 3 cloves garlic, minced
- 1/4 tsp. red pepper flakes
- 1 lemon, sliced
- 1 lemon, zested
- 1 tbsp. parsley, fresh, chopped

Directions:

1. Melt 1 tbsp. of butter in a large skillet over medium heat. Then, add in the mahi-mahi filets after seasoning with salt and pepper. Cook until lightly browned on each side. Remove and place on a platter.

2. In the same skillet, add 1 tablespoon of oil. Add in the asparagus and cook until soft. Season with salt and pepper and then move to plate. Add in 2 tbsp. butter and melt. Then, add in garlic and pepper flake and cook until fragrant. Now, you can add in the lemon, zest, juice, and parsley. Remove from heat and replace the fish and asparagus.

3. Spoon sauce over fish and then serve.

Serves: 4

Nutritional Facts: Calories: 200 | Proteins: 21g | Carbs: 0g | Fats: 6g

Tuscan Butter Shrimp

Ingredients:

- 2 tbsp. olive oil, extra-virgin
- 1 lb. shrimp, peeled, deveined (454g)
- Salt and pepper for taste
- 3 tbsp. butter
- 3 cloves garlic, minced
- 1/2 cup cherry tomatoes, quartered (76g)
- 3 cup baby spinach (327g)
- 1/2 cup heavy cream (118ml)
- 1/4 cup Parmesan, grated (27g)
- ¼ cup basil, fresh, chopped (21g)
- Lemon, cut into wedges

Directions:

1. Heat the oil in a large skillet over medium-high heat. Liberally season shrimp with salt and pepper and then add shrimp into the skillet. Cook shrimp until golden on both sides. Remove from skillet and set to the side.

2. Reduce heat and add in the butter. Once butter is melted, add in garlic and cook until fragrant. Then, add in tomatoes. Cook until tomatoes begin to burst. Then, add in spinach. When spinach has wilted, you can then add in the Parmesan, basil, and heavy cream. Simmer until sauce has slightly reduced and then return shrimp to skillet.

3. Cook until shrimp is warmed through, add more basil, and squeeze lemon over the skillet before serving.

Serves: 4   Nutritional Facts: Calories: 284 | Proteins: 26.1g | Carbs: 5.4g | Fats: 18.2g

Chili

Ingredients:

- 3 slices bacon, cut into strips
- 1/4 medium onion, chopped
- 2 celery stalks, chopped
- 1 bell pepper, green, chopped
- 1/2 cup mushrooms, sliced (76g)
- 2 cloves garlic, minced
- 2 lb. beef, ground (907g)
- 2 tbsp. chili powder
- 2 tsp. cumin, ground
- 2 tsp. oregano, dried
- 2 tbsp. paprika, smoked
- Salt and pepper for taste
- 2 cups beef broth, low-sodium (473ml)
- Sour cream
- Cheese, shredded
- Green onions, chopped
- Avocado, diced

Directions:

1. Cook bacon in a large skillet over medium heat. Remove when crisp and let drain on paper towels. Then, in the same skillet, add in onion, celery, pepper, and mushrooms and cook until tender. Then, add garlic and cook until fragrant. Remove vegetables and set to the side.

2. In the same skillet, add in meat and brown, breaking into small pieces as you go. Then, add in seasonings and the vegetable mix. Pour in broth and let simmer for 15 minutes. Then, ladle into bowls and serve with toppings of choice.

Serves: 8

Nutritional Facts: Calories: 442 | Proteins: 38.9g | Carbs: 12.1g | Fats: 27g

Zoodle Alfredo w/ Bacon

Ingredients:

- 1/2 lb. bacon, chopped (227g)
- 1 shallot, minced
- 1/4 cup white wine (59ml)
- 1 1/2 cup heavy cream (355ml)
- 1 container zucchini noodles
- Salt and pepper for taste

Directions:

1. Cook bacon in a skillet over medium heat until crisp. Remove and let drain on paper towels. Reserve some of the greases and then add the shallots into the skillet. Cook until soft and then add garlic. Cook until fragrant, add in wine, and let reduce down.

2. Add in the heavy cream and bring to a boil. Then, reduce heat and add in the Parmesan. Cook until sauce thickens. Then, add in the zoodles. Toss until coated with sauce. Remove from heat and add crisp bacon. Serve.

Serves: 4   Nutritional Facts: Calories: 504 | Proteins: 14.3g | Carbs: 31.9g | Fats: 37g

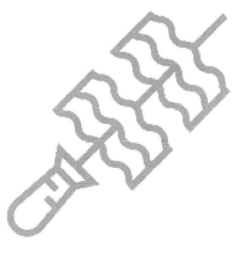

Cheesesteak-Stuffed Peppers

Ingredients:

- 4 bell peppers, halved
- 1 tbsp. vegetable oil
- 1 large onion, sliced
- 16 oz. mushrooms, sliced (454g)
- Salt and pepper for taste
- 1 1/2 lb. sirloin steak, sliced thin (680g)
- 2 tsp. Italian seasoning
- 16 slices provolone
- Parsley, fresh, chopped

Directions:

1. Preheat oven to 325 F (163 C). Add pepper to a large baking dish and bake for 30 minutes until soft. Heat the oil in a large skillet over medium-high heat. Then, add in onions and mushrooms. Season with salt and pepper and cook until tender.

2. Then, add in steak and mix in Italian seasoning and stir. Place a slice of provolone on the bottom of every pepper half. Then, add in the steak blend and top with another provolone slice. Bake for a few minutes until cheese has melted. Then, serve garnished with parsley.

Serves: 6

Nutritional Facts: Calories: 332 | Proteins: 50.1g | Carbs: 65g | Fats: 26g

Bacon-Wrapped Cauliflower

Ingredients:

- 1/4 cup olive oil, extra-virgin (59ml)
- 1/4 cup lemon juice, fresh (59ml)
- Salt for taste
- 1 head cauliflower
- 1 package frozen spinach, defrosted, squeezed
- 2 large eggs

- 4 green onions, sliced thin
- 2 cloves garlic, minced
- 3/4 cup cheddar, shredded (42g)
- 4 oz. cream cheese, softened, cubed
- 1/2 cup panko (53g)
- 1/4 cup Parmesan, grated (27g)

Directions:

1. Preheat oven to 450°F (204 C). Bring to a boil 8 cups water, oil, lemon juice, and 2 tablespoons of salt. Add cauliflower and bring back to a boil. Simmer until cauliflower is tender.

2. Remove cauliflower and place on a baking sheet. Let cool.

3. Add spinach, eggs, green onions, garlic, cheddar cheese, cream cheese, panko, and Parmesan into a food processor and combine. Then, place mixture in a piping bag and pipe mixture into all the crevices of the cauliflower. Then, wrap head with bacon.

4. Broil, rotating baking sheet part of the way through, until browned, around 30 minutes. Remove, let cool for a few minutes. Cut and serve.

Serves: 6　　　　　Nutritional Facts: Calories: 237 | Proteins: 19.2g | Carbs: 9.9g | Fats: 46.6g

Keto Jerk Chicken

Ingredients:

- 1 bundle green onions, sliced
- 2 cloves garlic, chopped
- 1 jalapeño, chopped
- 1 lime, juiced
- 2 tbsp. olive oil, extra-virgin
- 1 tbsp. brown sugar, packed
- 1/2 tsp. allspice, ground
- 1 tsp. thyme, dried
- 1/2 tsp. cinnamon, ground
- Salt for taste
- 8 chicken drumsticks and thighs, bone-in
- Vegetable oil

Directions:

1. Combine green onions, lime juice, garlic, jalapeno, oil, sugar, thyme, cinnamon, allspice, 1 teaspoon salt, and 2 tablespoons water in a blender and mix until smooth. Put aside ¼ cup.

2. Place chicken in a shallow dish and season with salt. Pour marinade over chicken, toss to coat. Let marinate overnight in the refrigerator.

3. Heat oiled grill pan on medium-high heat. Then, place chicken on the grill and turn once. Cook until both sides are browned and chicken is cooked. Move to a plate and brush with the remaining marinade. Then, serve garnished with green onions.

Serves: 4   Nutritional Facts: Calories: 43 | Proteins: .2g | Carbs: 4.3g | Fats: 3.1g

Keto Wrapped Dogs

Ingredients:

- 2 cup mozzarella, shredded (167g)
- 4 oz. cream cheese (113g)
- 2 large eggs
- 2 1/2 cup flour, almond (240g)
- 2 tsp. baking powder
- 1 tsp. salt
- 8 hot dogs
- 4 tbsp. butter, melted
- 1 tsp. garlic powder
- 1 tbsp. parsley, fresh, chopped
- Mustard

Directions:

1. Preheat stove to 400°F (204 C). Take parchment paper and line a baking sheet. Melt mozzarella and cream cheese in a microwavable safe bowl. In a large mixing bowl combine eggs, flour, baking powder, and salt.

2. Separate dough into 8 balls and then roll out each into a rope shape. Then, wrap around hot dogs. In a small bowl, mix together butter, garlic powder, and parsley. Then, brush over the top of the hot dog.

3. Bake in the oven until dough is golden. Remove from oven and serve with mustard.

Serves: 6   Nutritional Facts: Calories: 200 | Proteins: 14.5g | Carbs: 2.7g | Fats: 14.9g

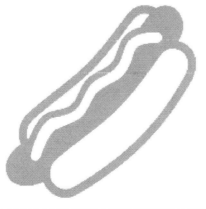

Jalapeno Popper-Stuffed Zucchini

Ingredients:

- 3 medium zucchini, halved
- 6 oz. cream cheese, softened (170g)
- 1/2 cup shredded mozzarella (42g)
- 1/2 cup cheddar, shredded (42g)
- 3 slices bacon, cooked and crumbled
- 1 jalapeno, minced
- 1 tsp. garlic powder
- Salt and pepper for taste
- 1 tbsp. parsley, fresh, chopped

Directions:

1. Preheat oven to 425°F (218 C). Trim zucchini and make several slices in the zucchini, not going all the way through. Then, place on a baking sheet lined with parchment paper. Bake in the oven until soft enough to separate slices more.

2. In a medium mixing bowl, add the cream cheese, 1/2 cup mozzarella, cheddar, bacon, jalapeño, and garlic powder. Season with salt and pepper and mix until thoroughly combined.

3. Remove zucchini and use jalapeno mix to stuff in between the slices. Then, bake until cheese is melted. Remove and serve with a garnish of parsley.

Serves: 6

Nutritional Facts: Calories: 198 | Proteins: 9.5g | Carbs: 2.2g | Fats: 17g

Skillet Chicken Buffalo-Style

Ingredients:

- 1 tbsp. olive oil, extra-virgin
- 4 chicken breast, boneless, skinless
- 1 tsp. garlic powder
- Salt and pepper for taste
- 2 tbsp. butter
- 2 cloves garlic, minced
- 1 cup buffalo sauce
- Pinch of cayenne pepper
- 8 slices muenster
- Chives, fresh, chopped

Directions:

1. Heat the oil in a large skillet over medium heat. Add in chicken and season with garlic powder, salt, and pepper. Cook until browned. Then, move to a plate.

2. In the same skillet, add butter and garlic. Cook until fragrant and then add in cayenne and buffalo sauce.

3. Then, place chicken back in the skillet. Top the chicken with cheese slices. Place lid on the skillet and let the cheese melt. Simmer chicken in sauce until cooked through. Then, serve garnished with chives.

Serves: 4   Nutritional Facts: Calories: 398 | Proteins: 14g | Carbs: 30.1g | Fats: 24.6g

SNACKS & DESSERTS

Black & White Fat Bomb

Ingredients:

- 2 cups almond, slivers
- 1 cup coconut, extra virgin
- 2 tbsp. powdered sweetener
- 2 tbsp. vanilla extract
- 1 tsp. orange zest
- Pinch of salt
- 2 tbsp. cocoa powder, unsweetened

Directions:

1. Line muffin tin with muffin cups. Then, add almonds, oil, sweetener, vanilla, zest, and salt into a food processor. Pulse until coarse. Place half in a small bowl and mix in cocoa powder.

2. Fill an equal amount of the muffin cups with each mixture.

3. Freeze for 30 minutes, store, or serve.

Serves: 12   Nutritional Facts: Calories: 164 | Proteins: .2g | Carbs: .8g | Fats: 18.4g

Chicken Buffalo Dip

Ingredients:

- 2 - 8 oz. packages cream cheese, reduced-fat, cut into little pieces (454g)
- 2 cups rotisserie chicken, shredded (273g)
- 2 cups cheese, cheddar, shredded (167g)
- 1 cup buttermilk (237g)
- 1/3 cup hot sauce (78g)
- 1 tbsp. flour, all-purpose
- 1 tsp. Worcestershire sauce
- 3/4 tsp. cayenne pepper
- 1 tsp. garlic powder
- 1 tsp. onion powder
- 1/2 cup parsley leaves, chopped (53g)
- 1/4 cup blue cheese, crumbled (43g)
- Celery and carrot sticks

Directions:

1. In a slow cooker, combine chicken, cream cheese, cheddar, hot sauce, buttermilk, flour, Worcestershire sauce, garlic powder, cayenne, and onion powder. Mix until thoroughly combined.

2. Cook, covered, on high for 2 hours. Mix until smooth. Sprinkle with parsley and blue cheese, reduce heat to warm, and serve with celery and carrot sticks.

Serves: 12

Nutritional Facts: Calories: 104 | Proteins: 8.5g | Carbs: 5g | Fats: 5.6g

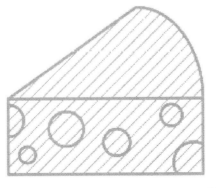

Bacon-Wrapped Shrimp & Scallops

Ingredients:

- 12 large shrimp, peeled, deveined
- 12 large scallops, cut and trimmed
- 1 lime, squeezed and zested
- 1 tbsp. toasted sesame oil
- 1 tbsp. salt and pepper
- 1 tsp. red pepper flakes
- 12 slices applewood smoked bacon, cut in 1/2
- 3 scallions, thinly sliced

Directions:

1. Preheat oven to 425 F (218 C). Place shrimp and scallops in a shallow dish. Squeeze the lime and sprinkle zest over seafood. Then, drizzle sesame oil, salt, pepper, and pepper flakes over the shrimp and scallops. Now, wrap a half slice of bacon around each portion and fasten with a toothpick.

2. Place shrimp on a grill over a baking sheet and bake in the oven for 10-14 minutes or until shrimp and scallops are cooked through. Then, serve garnished with scallions.

Serves: 12

Nutritional Facts: Calories: 123 | Proteins: 4.1g | Carbs: 1.2g | Fats: 11.4g

Olives Marinated in Citrus

Ingredients:

- 1/4 cup olive oil, extra-virgin (59ml)
- 1/4 tsp. red pepper flakes
- 2 sprigs thyme, fresh
- 1 clove garlic, chopped
- 1 strip lemon zest

- 1 tsp. lemon juice, fresh
- 1 strip orange zest
- 1 tbsp. orange juice
- Salt and pepper for taste
- 1 cup Castelvetrano olives (109g)

Directions:

1. Heat oil over medium heat in a small pot. Then, add red pepper flakes, orange zest, garlic, thyme, lemon zest, salt, and pepper for taste. Cook until the garlic is fragrant while stirring regularly. Mix in the olives and cook for about 2 minutes. Reduce heat and then squeeze the lemon and orange juice over the olives. Serve warm.

Serves: 6

Nutritional Facts: Calories: 64 | Proteins: .3g | Carbs: 2.4g | Fats: 6.3g

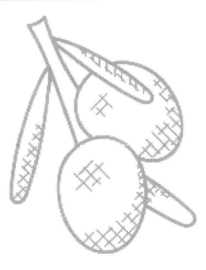

Chocolate Mug Cake

Ingredients:

- 2 tbsp. butter
- 1/4 cup flour, almond (24g)
- 2 tbsp. cocoa powder
- 1 large egg
- 2 tbsp. chocolate chips, sugar-free
- 1 tsp. substitute sweetener of choice
- 1/2 tsp. baking powder
- Pinch of salt
- ¼ cup whipped cream (54g)

Directions:

1. In a microwave-safe bowl, place butter and melt. Then, add the rest of the ingredients, excluding whipped cream. Stir until mixed. Cook for about 1 minute until cake is set.

2. Then, remove and serve topped with whipped cream.

Serves: 1

Nutritional Facts: Calories: 470 | Proteins: 15g | Carbs: 13g | Fats: 44g

Avocado Pops

Ingredients:

- 3 avocados, ripe
- 2 limes, juiced
- 3 tbsp. sugar alternative
- 3/4 cup coconut milk (177ml)
- 1 tbsp. coconut oil
- 1 cup chocolate chips, sugar-free (171g)

Directions:

1. Combine everything except chocolate chips and oil in a blender. Pulse until smooth. Then, pour into a popsicle mold. Place in the freezer.

2. Mix chips and oil in a medium microwave-safe bowl until melted. Then, dunk pops into the chocolate and serve.

Serves: 10

Nutritional Facts: Calories: 120 | Proteins: 1g | Carbs: 5g | Fats: 12g

Carrot Cake Balls

Ingredients:

- 1 block cream cheese, softened
- 3/4 cup flour, coconut (72g)
- 1 tsp. stevia
- 1/2 tsp. vanilla extract
- 1 tsp. cinnamon, ground
- 1/4 tsp. nutmeg, ground
- 1 cup carrots, grated (63g)
- 1/2 cup pecans, chopped (54g)
- 1 cup coconut, unsweetened, shredded (83g)

Directions:

1. Combine all ingredients together in a large mixing bowl except carrots and pecans. Once the mix is thoroughly combined, add in the carrots.

2. Roll into balls and roll in shredded coconut. Then, serve.

Serves: 16   Nutritional Facts: Calories: 74 | Proteins: 1.6g | Carbs: 2.8g | Fats: 6.6g

Peanut Butter Cheesecake Bites

Ingredients:

- 8 oz. cream cheese, softened (227g)
- 1/4 cup powdered alternative sweetener (50g)
- 1 tsp. vanilla extract
- 1/4 cup heavy whipping cream (59ml)
- 1/4 cup peanut butter (58g)
- 3/4 cup chocolate chips, sugar-free (128g)
- 2 tsp. coconut oil

Directions:

1. Blend cream cheese, alternative sweetener, and heavy whipping cream until smooth. Then, blend in peanut butter and vanilla extract until completely combined. Set to the side. Then, melt chocolate chips in oil.

2. Brush silicone cups with chocolate blend and refrigerate for 5 minutes. Repeat process for remaining cups.

3. Spoon in cream cheese mixture into each cup and place it in the freezer for 15 minutes. Then, top cups with more chocolate. Refrigerate for an hour and then serve.

Serves: 6   Nutritional Facts: Calories: 233 | Proteins: 4g | Carbs: 4g | Fats: 22g

BONUS 14-DAY MEAL PLAN

Day 1

Breakfast: *Blueberry Coconut Flour Porridge*

Ingredients:

- 1 cup almond milk (236ml)
- 1/4 cup flaxseed, ground (24g)
- 1/4 cup flour, coconut (24g)
- 1 tsp. cinnamon, ground
- 1 tsp. vanilla extract
- 10 drops stevia, liquid
- 1 pinch salt

Directions:

1. Over low heat, warm up almond milk.

2. Then, add flaxseed, flour, cinnamon, and salt. Stir, breaking up clumps. Bring to a simmer and add in vanilla extract and stevia.

3. Let the mixture thicken to porridge consistency and remove from heat. Serve with your choice of toppings.

Serves: 2   Nutritional Facts: Calories: 405 | Proteins: 10g | Carbs: 8g | Fats: 34g

Lunch: *Fish Cakes w/ Lemon Avocado Sauce (p-32)*

Dinner: *Fried Chicken (p-50)*

Day 2

Breakfast: *Asparagus & Bacon Frittata (p-11)*

Lunch: **Coconut Flour Tortillas**

Ingredients:

- 8 large egg whites
- 1/3 cup flour, coconut (40g)
- 10 tbsp. water
- 1/4 tsp. baking powder

- 1/4 tsp. garlic powder
- 1/4 tsp. onion powder
- 1/4 tsp. chili powder
- 1/4 tsp. salt

Directions:

1. Combine egg whites, coconut flour, baking powder, and water in a large mixing bowl and mix until thoroughly combined. Then, add in seasonings and mix again.

2. Heat a small skillet over a low heat. Once the skillet is hot, spray with cooking spray and add some of the batter into the skillet. Then, swirl the mixture until it coats the bottom of the skillet evenly. Let cook until air pockets begin to form and then flip. Cook another minute. Then, remove. Repeat with remaining batter. Use to make tacos, quesadillas, or burritos.

Serves: 16   Nutritional Facts: Calories: 50 | Proteins: 8.5g | Carbs: 6g | Fats: 1.5g

Dinner: *Meatballs in Sauce (p-52)*

Day 3

Breakfast: Ham w/ Bacon, Mushroom, & Cheese (p-12)

Lunch: Spiced Coconut Chicken (p-33)

Dinner: **Zucchini Pasta w/ Chicken & Pistachios**

Ingredients:

- 2 1/2 zucchini
- 1 tbsp. salt
- 1 tbsp. olive oil, extra-virgin
- 2 cloves, garlic
- ¼ tsp. cumin, ground
- 1/4 tsp. pepper
- 4 chicken breast, boneless, skinless

- 1 tbsp. olive oil, extra-virgin
- 1 tsp. salt
- 1/2 tsp. pepper
- 2 scallions
- 7-10 new mint leaves
- 1/4 cup pistachios, shelled
- 1 tbsp. lemon juice, fresh

Directions:

1. Spiralize the zucchini and place in a colander. Salt and let stand while preparing the other ingredients. Pound chicken out and then cut into strips. Heat oil in a nonstick skillet over medium-high heat. Season with salt and pepper and cook until browned on both sides. Remove the chicken and set to the side.

2. Cut scallions, mint, and pistachios. Combine in a bowl with lemon juice.

3. Place olive oil in a little bowl and add garlic (peeled and chopped). Then, add in the cumin and pepper. Wash the zucchini noodles under running water, dry them well. Return to the skillet you cooked the chicken and warm over medium-high heat and add to skillet. Sauté until tender. Then, add the garlic oil and reduce heat. Then, add the chicken back into the noodles and toss with mint/pistachio mixture. Remove from heat and serve.

Serves: 4   Nutritional Facts: Calories: 543 | Proteins: 8.1g | Carbs: 20g | Fats: 8.2g

Day 4

Breakfast: *Raspberry Cream Crepes*

Ingredients:

- Crepes
- 2 oz. cream cheese (57g)
- 2 eggs
- 2 tbsp. sugar substitute of choice
- Pinch of salt
- Dash of cinnamon
- Filling
- 2 1/2 tbsp. ricotta
- 3 oz. raspberries, frozen (85g)

1. Combine all crepe ingredients in a food processor. Pulse until cream cheese can't be seen.

2. Heat a skillet over medium heat until hot. Spray cooking spray into a skillet and pour a fourth of the batter into the skillet. While you›re pouring, tilt your skillet so that the crepe batter coats the entire bottom of the skillet in a thin layer.

3. Cook without touching the crepe until you see the underside getting brown and the top layer is set. Then, gently slide a spatula underneath the crepe and gently flip. Cook for 15 seconds. Repeat the process until batter is gone. Let crepes cool (do not lay on top of each other).

4. Once cooled, you can stuff. Take a little of the ricotta and place it in the center of the crepe. Then, add in raspberries. Roll crepe gently into a roll. Serve sprinkled with your favorite toppings.

Serves: 6   Nutritional Facts: Calories: 285 | Proteins: 8g | Carbs: 7g | Fats: 20g

Lunch: *Asian Meatballs w/ Vinaigrette (p-35)*

Dinner: *Garlicky Pork Chops w/ Rosemary (p-54)*

Day 5

Breakfast: *Frittata Stack (p-13)*
Lunch: **Cheeseburger Lettuce Wraps**

Ingredients:

Patties

- 2 lbs. beef, ground (907g)
- 1/2 tsp. seasoned salt
- 1 tsp. pepper
- 1 tsp. oregano, dried
- 6 slices cheese
- 2 large heads of romaine

- 2 tomatoes, sliced
- 1 small onion, sliced

Sauce

- 1/4 cup mayo, light (54g)
- 3 tbsp. ketchup
- 1 tbsp. relish, dill
- Dash of salt and pepper

Directions:

1. Heat a skillet over medium heat. Mix beef, seasoned salt, pepper, and oregano in a large mixing bowl. Form small balls and then press those into patty shapes. Then, add to heated skillet and cook for about 4 minutes per side or until done enough for you.

2. In a small mixing bowl, combine all the sauce ingredients and stir until combined thoroughly. Set in refrigerator until ready to use.

3. Place a cheese slice on the burger and then place it on a lettuce leaf. Spread sauce, add other toppings over the top and wrap leaf around burger.

Serves: 4   Nutritional Facts: Calories: 719 | Proteins: 73g | Carbs: 25g | Fats: 37g

Dinner: *Taco Casserole (p-55)*

Day 6

Breakfast: *Florentine Casserole (p-15)*

Lunch: *Tortilla Espanola (p-36)*

Dinner: **Shrimp w/ Cauliflower Grits**

Ingredients:

- 1 lb. shrimp, peeled, deveined (454g)
- 1 tbsp. paprika
- 2 tsp. garlic powder
- 1/2 tsp. cayenne pepper
- 2 tbsp. olive oil, extra-virgin
- Salt and pepper for taste

- 1 tbsp. butter, unsalted
- 4 cups cauliflower, riced (546g)
- 1 cup milk, whole (237ml)
- 1/2 cup goat cheese, crumbled (75g)
- 3 cloves, garlic, chopped
- 4 cups baby arugula (607g)

Directions:

1. Put shrimp in a freezer bag. Then, in a small mixing bowl, combine the garlic powder, paprika, and cayenne until thoroughly combined. Place seasonings in bag with shrimp. Refrigerate.

2. Melt butter over medium heat and then add in the cauliflower rice. Cook until liquid is reduced. Then, mix in half the milk and bring to a boil. Stir until milk reduces by half and let thicken. Then, mix in goat cheese and season with salt and pepper. Keep warm.

3. Heat the oil in a large skillet over medium heat. Add in garlic and sauté until fragrant. Then, add in arugula and cook until wilted. Season with salt and pepper. Then, remove and let stand.

4. Heat the olive oil over medium heat in a large skillet. Then, add in shrimp and cook until cooked through. Season with salt and pepper. Serve.

Serves: 4   Nutritional Facts: Calories: 308 | Proteins: 24g | Carbs: 13g | Fats: 18g

Day 7

Breakfast: *Coconut Macadamia Bars*

Ingredients:

- 60g macadamia nuts
- 1/2 cup almond butter(125g)
- 1/4 cup oil, coconut (55g)
- 6 tbsp. coconut, shredded, unsweetened
- 20 drops stevia

Directions:

1. Add macadamia nuts into a food processor and pulse until chopped.

2. Add in butter, oil, and coconut into a large mixing bowl. Then, pour in nuts and add stevia.

3. Combine the mixture thoroughly and layer onto a parchment-lined baking dish. Refrigerate overnight, slice, and serve.

Serves: 6   Nutritional Facts: Calories: 327 | Proteins: 5g | Carbs: 7g | Fats: 33g

Lunch: *Zucchini Noodles w/ Shrimp (p-37)*

Dinner: *Meatloaf (p-57)*

Day 8

Breakfast: *Quiche Cups w/ Broccoli (p-17)*

Lunch: Chocolate Coconut Smoothie Bowl

Ingredients:

- 3/4 cup coconut milk (177ml)
- 2 tbsp. cacao powder, raw
- 15 drops stevia
- Ice, a hand full
- 2 scoops collagen protein

Directions:

1. Combine all ingredients, excluding the collagen, in a blender and pulse until completely combined.

2. Then, add the collagen in and pulse gently. Fill bowl and top with garnishes of your choice.

Serves: 1   Nutritional Facts: Calories: 500 | Proteins: 26g | Carbs: 12g | Fats: 38g

Dinner: *Lemon Garlic Mahi-Mahi (p-59)*

Day 9

Breakfast: Oven-Baked Denver Omelette (p-18)

Lunch: Cucumber Avocado Chicken Salad (p-38)

Dinner: **Garlic Butter Brazilian Steak**

Ingredients:

- 6 cloves garlic, chopped
- Salt and pepper for taste
- 1.5 lb. skirt steak cut into 4 pcs. (680g)
- 2 tbsp. vegetable oil
- 2 oz. butter, unsalted (57g)
- 1 tbsp. parsley, fresh, chopped

Directions:

1. Crush garlic and salt while mincing. Pat the steak dry and then season generously on both sides of steak. Heat the oil in a large skillet over medium-high heat. Cook until steak is seared on both sides. Then, remove from skillet and let rest.

2. Melt butter in a small skillet over low heat. Add garlic and cook until fragrant. Then, cut steak and plate. Spoon garlic butter over the steak and serve garnished with parsley.

Serves: 4

Nutritional Facts: Calories: 429 | Proteins: 37g | Carbs: 2g | Fats: 31g

Day 10

Breakfast: *Macadamia Berry Blast Granola*

Ingredients:

- 4 oz. macadamia nuts (113g)
- 4 oz. almonds, sliced (113g)
- 2 oz. cacao nibs (57g)
- 1 1/2 oz. coconut, unsweetened, flaked (43g)
- 1/2 cup strawberries, freeze-dried (54g)
- 2 tbsp. coconut oil
- 1 large egg white
- 1/4 cup brown sugar alternative (49g)
- Pinch of salt

Directions:

1. Preheat oven to 325 F (163 C). Line a large baking sheet with parchment paper. Chop the macadamia nuts and almonds into pieces.

2. Combine all the ingredients except the egg white, strawberries, and coconut flakes together in a large mixing bowl. At that point, include the egg white mixture until the mixture is coated.

3. Pour the granola onto baking sheet and spread out. Place in oven and bake for 15-25 minutes or just until it is fragrant and toasted. Let cool completely and then mix in coconut flakes and strawberries.

4. Store in a container that is air-tight.

Serves: 8   Nutritional Facts: Calories: 297 | Proteins: 6g | Carbs: 16g | Fats: 27g

Lunch: *Low Carb Cauliflower Salad (p-39)*

Dinner: *Tuscan Butter Shrimp (p-60)*

Day 11

Breakfast: *Scrambled Eggs w/ Avocado (p-19)*

Lunch: **Taco Stuffed Avocado**

Ingredients:

- 4 avocados
- 1 lime, juiced
- 1 tbsp. olive oil, extra virgin
- 1 medium onion, chopped
- 1 lb. beef, ground (454g)
- 1 packet taco seasoning

- Salt and pepper for taste
- 2/3 cup cheese, shredded (55g)
- 1/2 cup lettuce, shredded (42g)
- 1/2 cup grape tomatoes, quartered (75g)
- Sour cream

Directions:

1. Halve the avocados and spoon some of the avocados out, making the pit bigger. Take the excess avocado and dice up. Drizzle lime juice over the top.

2. Heat oil in a medium skillet over medium heat. Then, add in beef and taco seasoning and brown, breaking the meat up as you mix. Season with salt and pepper. Once browned, remove from heat and drain off fat.

3. Take the beef mixture and fill the avocados with it. Then, top with the toppings and serve.

Serves: 8   Nutritional Facts: Calories: 336 | Proteins: 19.6g | Carbs: 12.3g | Fats: 24.5g

Dinner: *Chili (p-62)*

Day 12

Breakfast: *Eggs & Bacon Bundles (p-20)*

Lunch: *Egg Salad w/ Avocado (p-41)*

Dinner: **Blackened Salmon w/ Avocado Salsa**

Ingredients:

- 1 tbsp. oil
- 4 pieces of salmon
- 4 tsp. Cajun flavoring
- 4 avocado, diced
- 1/4 cup onion, red, diced (43g)
- 1 jalapeno, diced
- 1 tbsp. cilantro, chopped
- 1 tbsp. lime juice, fresh
- salt to taste
- 1 cup cucumber, diced (152g)
- 1/4 cup green onion, diced (18g)
- 1 tbsp. parsley, cleaved
- 1 tbsp. lemon juice, fresh

Directions:

1. Heat a large skillet with oil over medium-high heat. Then, add in the salmon and season with Cajun seasoning. Cook salmon until golden brown on both sides.

2. Combine avocado, red onion, jalapeno, cilantro, and lime juice. Mix well and then salt to taste.

3. Combine avocado, cucumber, parsley, lemon juice, and salt for taste.

4. Serve salmon with the salsa spooned over top.

Serves: 4

Nutritional Facts: Calories: 445 | Proteins: 35.1g | Carbs: 9.8g | Fats: 31.3g

Day 13

Breakfast: *Low Carb Pancakes*

Ingredients:

- 50g protein powder, vanilla
- 2 tsp. baking powder
- 1 pinch salt
- 1 tbsp. flour, coconut
- 2 eggs
- 1/4 tsp. vanilla extract
- 4 tbsp. butter, unsalted
- 1 tbsp. heavy cream

Directions:

1. Combine all dry ingredients and set them to the side. Then, combine all wet ingredients and then pour wet ingredients into dry. Mix well with a spoon until all ingredients are combined.

2. Heat a large skillet with oil and then ladle in the batter.

3. Cook until bubbles form on top and then flip with a spatula. Repeat with the rest of the batter. Then, serve with toppings of your choice.

Serves: 2   Nutritional Facts: Calories: 500 | Proteins: 38g | Carbs: 1g | Fats: 37g

Lunch: *Green Bean & Roasted Fennel Salad (p-42)*

Dinner: *Zoodles Alfredo w/ Bacon (p-63)*

Day 14

Breakfast: *Greek-Inspired Breakfast Casserole (p-21)*

Lunch: **Caprese Zoodles**

Ingredients:

- 4 large zucchini
- 2 tbsp. olive oil, extra virgin
- Salt and pepper for taste
- 2 cups cherry tomatoes, halved (300g)
- 1 cup mozzarella balls, quartered (182g)
- 1/4 cup basil, fresh, chopped (27g)
- 2 tbsp. vinegar, balsamic

Directions:

1. Create zucchini noodles with a spiralizer. Then, add into a large mixing bowl and coat with olive oil and season with salt and pepper. Let sit for about 15 minutes.

2. Then, add in tomatoes, mozzarella, and basil to the zoodles. Then, drizzle with vinegar and serve.

Serves: 4   Nutritional Facts: Calories: 190 | Proteins: 10.1g | Carbs: 30.1g | Fats: 3.4g

Dinner: *Cheesesteak-Stuffed Pepper (p-64)*

EXCLUSIVE BONUS!

Get Keto Audiobook for FREE NOW!*

*The Ultimate Keto Diet Guide 2019-2020:
How to Loose weight with Quick and Easy Steps*

SCAN ME

or go to

www.free-keto.co.uk

Disclaimer

The opinions and ideas of the author contained in this publication are designed to educate the reader in an informative and helpful manner. While we accept that the instructions will not suit every reader, it is only to be expected that the recipes might not gel with everyone. Use the book responsibly and at your own risk. This work with all its contents, does not guarantee correctness, completion, quality or correctness of the provided information. Always check with your medical practitioner should you be unsure whether to follow a low carb eating plan. Misinformation or misprints cannot be completely eliminated. Human error is real!

Design: Oliviaprodesign

Picture: Larisa Blinova / www.shutterstock.com

Printed in Great Britain
by Amazon